BATHROOM TRIVIA

FUN AND EASY QUIZ QUESTIONS

© 2023 E.S. Carruthers

ISBN: 9798389245723

Imprint: Independently published

Imprint: Independently published

1. What is the national animal of Australia?
Kangaroo/Koala

2. What is the largest species of bear?
Polar bear/Black bear

3. How many legs does a spider have?
Eight/Ten

4. Scientific name for the African elephant? Loxodonta africana/Elephas maximus

5. Animal is known for its black and white stripes? Zebra/Tiger

6. What is the largest species of snake?
Anaconda/Boa constrictor

7. National bird of the United States?
Bald eagle/Wild turkey

8. What is the only bear native to South America?
Spectacled bear/Sun bear

9. What bird mimics human speech?
Parrot, owl

10. What is the largest living species of reptile? Anaconda/Komodo dragon

ANSWERS:

1- The *Kangaroo* is the national animal of Australia. The Australian kangaroo is the largest marsupial in the world, with males standing up to 6 feet (1.8 meters) tall and weighing as much as 200 pounds (90 kilograms).

2- The *Polar bear* is the largest species of bear. Polar bears are the largest land predator in the world, with adult males weighing up to 1,500 pounds (680 kilograms) and standing over 10 feet (3 meters) tall when on their hind legs.

3- A spider has *eight* legs. Spiders use venom to liquefy their prey's insides, which they then suck up through their straw-like mouthparts called chelicerae.
The pronunciation of the word "chelicerae" is "keh-lih-seh-ree".

4- *Loxodonta africana* is the scientific name for the African elephant. The African elephant is the largest land animal on earth, with males weighing up to 12,000 pounds (5,400 kg) and standing up to 13 feet (4 meters) tall at the shoulder. Elephants also have the largest brain of any land animal, weighing up to 12 pounds (5.5 kg). African elephants are known for their intelligence, social complexity, and long memories, which can span several decades. They are also important ecosystem engineers, shaping their environment through their feeding and movement patterns.

5- The *Zebra* is known for its black and white stripes. A fact about zebra stripes is that their unique pattern may serve as a natural insect repellent, as the stripes may interfere with the visual perception of biting flies, such as horseflies and tsetse flies.

6- The *Anaconda* is the largest species of snake. The Anaconda can reach lengths of up to 30 feet (9 meters) and weigh up to 550 pounds (250 kilograms).

7- The *Bald eagle* is the national bird of the United States. Its name comes from the old English word "balde," meaning white-headed, which describes the eagle's distinctive white-feathered head.

8- *The Spectacled bear is the only species of bear native to South America.* The Spectacled bear is the smallest bear species in the world. Despite their name, they do not actually have spectacles or glasses-like markings around their eyes - instead, they have distinctive beige or white fur around their eyes that may create the appearance of spectacles.

9- *The Parrot is known for its ability to mimic human speech*. Parrots are highly intelligent birds and are capable of using and understanding language. Some species of parrots, such as the African Grey Parrot, are known to have vocabularies of up to several hundred words and can even use them in context to communicate with humans. Additionally, parrots are known for their ability to mimic sounds and even the voices of humans and other animals.

10- The largest living species of reptile is the _Komodo dragon_. The Komodo dragon is the world's largest lizard species, capable of growing up to 10 feet in length and weighing up to 200 pounds. They are also known for their powerful jaws, sharp teeth, and toxic saliva, which they use to hunt and kill their prey, including deer, water buffalo, and even humans. Despite their fearsome reputation, Komodo dragons are actually very vulnerable to extinction due to habitat loss and poaching.

Zebras actually have black skin with white stripes.

1- Who painted the famous artwork "The Starry Night"?
a) Vincent van Gogh
b) Pablo Picasso

2- Which Renaissance artist painted the ceiling of the Sistine Chapel in Vatican City?
a) Michelangelo
b) Sandro Botticelli

3- Characterized by bright colors and bold brushstrokes, and included artists such as Henri Matisse and André Derain?
a) Cubism
b) Fauvism

4- Who sculpted the famous statue "David"?
a) Michelangelo
b) Donatello

5- Which artist is known for his iconic painting "Campbell's Soup Cans"?
a) Andy Warho
b) Jackson Pollock

6- Known for its emphasis on capturing the fleeting impressions of light and color in a scene?
a) Impressionism
b) Realism

7- Who painted the mural "The Last Supper"?
a) Leonardo da Vinci
b) Michelangelo

8- Characterized by the use of geometric shapes and primary colors?
a) Futurism
b) De Stijl

9- Who sculpted the famous statue "The Thinker"?
a) Auguste Rodin
b) Salvador Dalí

10- Which art style, characterized by distorted figures and vivid colors, was popularized by artists such as Salvador Dalí and René Magritte?
a) Surrealism
b) Impressionism

1- Vincent van Gogh painted the famous artwork "The Starry Night. Van Gogh sold only one painting during his lifetime, despite producing over 900 paintings and 1,100 drawings over the course of his career. The painting he sold was "The Red Vineyard," which he sold to Anna Boch in 1890 for 400 francs. Today, Van Gogh is considered one of the most famous and influential artists in history, and his works sell for millions of dollars at auctions around the world.

2- Michelangelo painted the ceiling of the Sistine Chapel in Vatican City.
Michelangelo was not only a renowned painter but also a skilled sculptor, architect, and poet. Some of his most famous works include the ceiling frescoes of the Sistine Chapel in Rome, the sculpture of David in Florence, and the dome of St. Peter's Basilica in Vatican City. Michelangelo is widely regarded as one of the greatest

artists of all time, and his works have had a profound influence on the art and culture of Western civilization.

3- Fauvism was characterized by bright colors and bold brushstrokes. Fauvism was a short-lived art movement that emerged in France in the early 20th century. The term "Fauvism" comes from the French word "fauves," meaning "wild beasts," and was used by art critic Louis Vauxcelles to describe the bright and bold colors used by Fauvist artists such as Henri Matisse and André Derain. Fauvism was characterized by its use of intense colors and simplified forms to create a sense of emotional intensity and expressionism, and it had a significant influence on the development of modern art.

4- Michelangelo sculpted the famous statue "David". "David" was created between 1501 and 1504, and it stands at 17 feet tall (5.17 meters) in Florence, Italy.

5- Andy Warhol is known for his iconic painting "Campbell's Soup Cans". Warhol is also known for his portraits of celebrities like Marilyn Monroe and Elvis Presley. Warhol's work challenged traditional ideas about art and popular culture, and his legacy continues to influence contemporary art and culture today.

6- Impressionism is known for its emphasis on capturing the fleeting impressions of light. Impressionism was a 19th-century art movement that originated in France. The Impressionists, including artists such as Claude Monet, Pierre-Auguste Renoir, and Edgar Degas, sought to capture the fleeting and ephemeral effects of light and color in their paintings. They often painted outdoors, or en plein air, and used loose brushwork and bright colors to convey the sensory experience of a moment. The Impressionists were initially criticized by the art establishment but eventually became some of the most celebrated and influential artists in history.

7- Leonardo da Vinci painted the famous mural "The Last Supper". Leonardo da Vinci was a true Renaissance man, excelling in multiple fields such as painting, sculpture, architecture, science, engineering, and anatomy. He is perhaps best known for creating some of the most iconic artworks in history, including the Mona Lisa and The Last Supper. However, he was also an accomplished inventor, designing prototypes for flying machines, war machines, and various other inventions ahead of his time. His works continue to inspire and fascinate people around the world, and he is widely regarded as one of the most brilliant minds in history.

8- De Stijl is characterized by the use of geometric shapes. De Stijl was an artistic movement founded in the Netherlands in 1917 by a group of artists and designers, including Piet Mondrian, Theo van Doesburg, and Gerrit Rietveld. The movement was characterized by the use of primary colors, straight lines, and rectangular shapes, and sought to create a universal aesthetic language that would reflect the modern age. De Stijl had a significant impact on modern art and design, and its influence can still be seen in architecture, graphic design, and other areas of visual culture today. "Stijl" is a Dutch word and it is pronounced as "stayl" in English.

9- Auguste Rodin sculpted the famous statue "The Thinker". Auguste Rodin was a French sculptor who is widely considered to be one of the greatest artists of the modern era. He is best known for his bronze statue "The Thinker," which depicts a man deep in thought, and his marble sculpture "The Kiss," which shows a couple locked in a passionate embrace. Rodin's work was controversial in its time, as he often departed from traditional artistic conventions and portrayed the human form in a more realistic and expressive way. Despite this, his work was highly influential and paved the way for many modernist and avant-garde artists who followed him. "Auguste" is a French name, and it is pronounced as "oh-guhst" in English.

10- Surrealism is characterized by distorted figures and vivid colors and was popularized by artists such as Salvador Dalí and René Magritte.

Surrealism was an artistic and literary movement that emerged in the early 20th century, led by the French writer André Breton. The movement sought to unlock the power of the unconscious mind, and its works were characterized by a dreamlike quality, unexpected juxtapositions, and irrational imagery.

Surrealist art often featured bizarre, unsettling, or fantastical scenes, and its artists drew on techniques such as automatism, collage, and photomontage to create their works. Surrealism had a significant impact on modern art, literature, and culture, and its influence can still be seen in contemporary art today.

1- What is the name of the famous Egyptian pyramid in Giza?
 a) The Sphinx Pyramid
 b) The Great Pyramid of Giza

2- What famous skyscraper in New York City was designed by architect William Van Alen?
 a) Empire State Building
 b) Chrysler Building

3- What is the name of the famous Italian architect who designed the dome of St. Peter's Basilica in Vatican City?
 a) Filippo Brunelleschi
 b) Michelangelo

4- What is the name of the famous French architect who designed the Eiffel Tower?
 a) Gustave Eiffel
 b) Charles Garnier

5- What is the name of the famous American architect who designed the Guggenheim Museum in New York City?
 a) Frank Gehry
 b) Richard Meier

6- Who designed the glass pyramid at the entrance of the Louvre Museum in Paris?
 a) Richard Rogers
 b) I.M. Pei

7- What is the name of the famous Japanese architect who designed the Tokyo Skytree?
 a) Kenzo Tange
 b) Tadao Ando

8- What is the name of the famous Indian architect who designed the Lotus Temple in New Delhi?
 a) B.V. Doshi
 b) Charles Correa

9- What is the name of the famous Spanish architect who designed the iconic Sagrada Familia church in Barcelona?

a) Santiago Calatrava
b) Antoni Gaudi

Answers:

1- The Great Pyramid of Giza is the name of the famous Egyptian pyramid in Giza. The Great Pyramid of Giza was built around 2560 BC as a tomb for the Pharaoh Khufu and stands at a height of 147 meters (481 feet), making it the tallest man-made structure in the world at the time of its construction.

The pyramid is made up of over 2 million limestone blocks, each weighing an average of 2.5 tons, and its interior contains a series of corridors, chambers, and ventilation shafts. Despite being over 4,500 years old, the Great Pyramid of Giza remains one of the most impressive and enigmatic structures in the world, attracting millions of visitors every year.

2- The Empire State Building was designed by architect William Van Alen.

The Empire State Building is a famous skyscraper located in New York City, USA. It was completed in 1931 and stands at a height of 443 meters (1,454 feet), making it one of the tallest buildings in the world.

At the time of its construction, the Empire State Building was the tallest building in the world and held this title for over 40 years until the completion of the World Trade Center in 1972.

The building has 102 floors and is made up of steel and concrete. It is also known for its distinctive Art Deco style, which includes decorative motifs such as setbacks, terraces, and spires. The Empire State Building remains an iconic symbol of New York City and attracts millions of visitors each year.

3- Michelangelo designed the dome of St. Peter's Basilica in Vatican City. St. Peter's Basilica is a major basilica located in Vatican City, an independent city-state within Rome, Italy. It is considered one of the holiest Catholic shrines and is regarded as one of the greatest works of Renaissance architecture. The basilica was designed by some of the most prominent architects of the time, including Michelangelo, Bramante, and Bernini, and it took over 120 years to complete.

The dome of St. Peter's Basilica, which was designed by Michelangelo, is one of the most recognizable features of the structure and is the tallest dome in the world, standing at a height of 136 meters (446 feet). The basilica is also home to numerous works of art, including Michelangelo's famous sculpture, the Pietà. Today, St. Peter's Basilica is visited by millions of tourists and pilgrims each year.

4- Gustave Eiffel designed the Eiffel Tower. The Eiffel Tower is a famous landmark located in Paris, France. It was designed by Gustave Eiffel and was built as the entrance arch to the 1889 World's Fair. At the time of its construction, it was the tallest man-made structure in the world, standing at a height of 300 meters (984 feet).

The tower is made of wrought iron and consists of four pillars that join together to form a single tower. It has become a symbol of Paris and is one of the most visited tourist attractions in the world, with millions of visitors each year. Interestingly, the Eiffel Tower was originally intended to be a temporary structure and was almost dismantled after the World's Fair, but it was ultimately saved due to its usefulness as a radio antenna.

5- Frank Gehry designed the Guggenheim Museum in New York City.
The Guggenheim Museum is a renowned modern and contemporary art museum located in New York City, USA. It was designed by the famous architect Frank Lloyd Wright and was completed in 1959. The museum is famous for its distinctive spiral design, with a central rotunda surrounded by a continuous ramp that spirals upward over the course of several floors.

The Guggenheim's collection includes works by some of the most significant artists of the 20th and 21st centuries, including Pablo Picasso, Wassily Kandinsky, Jackson Pollock, and many others. Today, the Guggenheim Museum is recognized as one of the most important institutions for modern and contemporary art in the world, and it has branches in several other cities, including Bilbao, Spain, and Abu Dhabi, United Arab Emirates.

6- I.M. Pei designed the glass pyramid at the entrance of the Louvre Museum in

Paris. The Louvre Museum is the largest art museum in the world, with a collection of over 380,000 objects and 35,000 works of art on display in an area of over 782,000 square feet. It is also one of the most visited museums in the world, with approximately 10 million visitors annually.

7- Kenzo Tange designed the Tokyo Skytree. The Tokyo Skytree is the tallest tower in the world and the second-tallest structure in the world after the Burj Khalifa in Dubai. The Tokyo Skytree stands at a height of 634 meters (2,080 feet) and serves as a broadcasting tower and observation deck for tourists. It is a popular tourist attraction in Tokyo, Japan, and offers panoramic views of the cityscape from its observation decks located at 350 and 450 meters above ground level.

8- B.V. Doshi designed the Lotus Temple in New Delhi. The Lotus Temple, located in Delhi, India, is inspired by the lotus flower, which is considered a sacred symbol in Hinduism, Buddhism, and Jainism.

The temple is shaped like a half-open lotus flower, with 27 free-standing marble petals arranged in groups of three to form nine sides. The structure, which opened to the public in 1986, is made of white marble and is surrounded by nine ponds and gardens.

The Lotus Temple is open to people of all faiths and is one of the most visited religious sites in the world, attracting over 70 million visitors since its opening.

9- Antoni Gaudi designed the iconic Sagrada Familia church in Barcelona.
The Sagrada Familia church in Barcelona, Spain, has been under construction for over 138 years and is still not completed. The construction of the church began in 1882 and is expected to be completed in 2026, which will mark the 100th death anniversary of the architect Antoni Gaudi, who designed the church. The Sagrada Familia church is known for its unique and intricate design, which combines elements of Gothic and Art Nouveau architecture. It is also a UNESCO World Heritage Site and one of the most popular tourist attractions in Barcelona, with over 4 million visitors annually.

1- Who invented the light bulb?
a) Thomas Edison
b) Benjamin Franklin

2- First president of the United States?
a) George Washington
b) Abraham Lincoln

3- What was the first country to declare independence from the British Empire?
a) United States
b) India

4- Which ancient civilization built the pyramids?
a) Greeks
b) Egyptians

5- Who was the first person to circumnavigate the globe?
a) Christopher Columbus
b) Ferdinand Magellan

6- What was the name of the first successful manned mission to the Moon?
a) Apollo 11
b) Gemini 4

7- Who was the first female prime minister of the United Kingdom?
a) Margaret Thatcher
b) Angela Merkel

8- Who was the first person to discover America?
a) Christopher Columbus
b) Leif Erikson

9- In what year did World War II end?
a) 1945
b) 1950

10- Who wrote the Declaration of Independence?
a) George Washington
b) Thomas Jefferson

ANSWERS:

1- Who invented the light bulb?
Thomas Edison Thomas Edison held over 1,000 patents for his inventions, including the phonograph, the motion picture camera, and the practical electric light bulb.

Edison was a prolific inventor and his contributions to science and technology had a profound impact on the modern world.

He is also credited with developing the first research and development (R&D) laboratory, which was known as the "Invention Factory" and was located in Menlo Park, New Jersey. Edison's work and legacy continue to inspire innovation and creativity in fields such as science, engineering, and entrepreneurship.

**2- The first president of the United States?
George Washington** George Washington
was the only U.S. president to be
unanimously elected. In 1789, Washington
was elected as the first president of the
United States, with all 69 electors casting
their votes in his favor.

Washington was widely respected and
admired for his leadership during the
American Revolution and his role in shaping
the new nation's government.

He served two terms as president and
helped to establish many of the traditions
and practices of the presidency that are still
in use today, such as the inaugural address
and the use of the title "Mr. President."

3- What was the first country to declare independence from the British Empire? United States. The British Empire was the largest empire in history, with territories and colonies spanning across every continent at its peak in the early 20th century. It was also the first truly global empire, with a reach that extended far beyond Europe and included Africa, Asia, Australia, and the Americas.

The British Empire played a significant role in shaping the modern world, spreading English language, culture, and legal systems across the globe. However, it also involved the exploitation and oppression of many peoples and contributed to ongoing political and social issues in some regions even after its dissolution.

4- Which civilization built the pyramids?
Egyptians. The Egyptian pyramids were built
during the Old Kingdom period, approximately
between 2686 and 2181 BCE, as tombs for
pharaohs and their consorts.

The largest and most famous pyramids, such as
the Great Pyramid of Giza, were constructed using
millions of limestone and granite blocks weighing
up to 80 tons each. The precise methods used by
the ancient Egyptians to build these massive
structures remain a mystery, but it is believed that
they used ramps, pulleys, and levers to move and
position the stones. The pyramids continue to be a
symbol of ancient Egyptian civilization and attract
millions of visitors each year.

**5- First to circumnavigate the globe?
Ferdinand Magellan.** Ferdinand Magellan
was a Portuguese explorer who led the first
expedition that circumnavigated the globe,
although he himself did not complete the
journey as he was killed in a battle in the
Philippines.

**6- The first manned mission to the Moon?
Apollo 11.** Apollo 11 was launched on July
16, 1969, and the lunar module, Eagle,
landed on the Moon's surface on July 20,
1969. Neil Armstrong, the mission
commander, became the first human to
step on the Moon and famously declared,
"That's one small step for man, one giant
leap for mankind."

7- The first female prime minister of the United Kingdom?
Margaret Thatcher. Margaret Thatcher, also known as the "Iron Lady," was the first female Prime Minister of the United Kingdom, serving from 1979 to 1990. She was known for her conservative policies and tough stance on foreign relations, and was a major figure in British politics during the Cold War. Thatcher was also the longest-serving British prime minister of the 20th century.

8- The first person to discover America?
Leif Erikson. Leif Erikson was a Norse explorer who is believed to have been the first European to set foot on North American soil, almost 500 years before Christopher Columbus. He established a Norse settlement in present-day Newfoundland, Canada, which he called Vinland, around the year 1000 AD.

9- In what year did World War II end?
1945. One of the most significant events of

1945 was the end of World War II. The war ended with the unconditional surrender of Germany on May 8, 1945, which is celebrated as Victory in Europe Day (VE Day).

However, the war continued in the Pacific theater until August 15, 1945, when Japan announced its surrender after the atomic bombings of Hiroshima and Nagasaki by the United States. This led to the formal end of the war on September 2, 1945, which is celebrated as Victory over Japan Day (VJ Day).

10- Who wrote the Declaration of Independence?

Thomas Jefferson Thomas Jefferson, the third President of the United States, was the principal author of the Declaration of Independence, which was adopted by the Continental Congress on July 4, 1776.

1- Who invented the telephone?
a) Alexander Graham Bell
b) Thomas Edison

2- First person to reach the North Pole?
a) Robert Peary
b) Frederick Cook

3- Who was the first person to fly solo across the Atlantic Ocean?
a) Charles Lindbergh
b) Amelia Earhart

4- Wrote the novel "War and Peace"?
a) Leo Tolstoy
b) Fyodor Dostoevsky

5- Who was the first emperor of Rome?
a) Julius Caesar
b) Augustus Caesar

ANSWERS

1- Who invented the telephone?
Alexander Graham Bell. Alexander Graham Bell, a Scottish-born inventor and scientist, is best known for inventing the telephone in 1876. However, he also made important contributions to other fields, such as speech therapy for the deaf, aviation, and hydrofoils. Bell was also one of the founding members of the National Geographic Society.

2- First person to reach the North Pole?
Robert Peary. Robert Peary was an American explorer who is best known for claiming to be the first person to reach the geographic North Pole.

However, his claim has been disputed, and some experts believe that he may not have actually reached the North Pole. Regardless, Peary made several important expeditions to the Arctic, and he was awarded the Medal of Honor for his efforts in the field of exploration.

3- Who was the first person to fly solo across the Atlantic Ocean?
Charles Lindbergh Charles Lindbergh was an American aviator who became the first person to fly solo across the Atlantic Ocean in 1927. He made the historic flight in a single-engine monoplane called the Spirit of St. Louis, which he had helped design. The flight took 33.5 hours and covered a distance of over 3,600 miles, from New York to Paris. Lindbergh's achievement earned him widespread fame and acclaim, and he became an important figure in the history of aviation.

4- Wrote the novel "War and Peace"?
Leo Tolstoy Leo Tolstoy was a Russian
writer and philosopher who is widely
regarded as one of the greatest authors in
history. He is best known for his novels War
and Peace and Anna Karenina, which are
considered masterpieces of world literature.
Tolstoy's writing explored themes such as
love, family, morality, and the human
condition. In addition to his literary works,
Tolstoy was also known for his pacifist
beliefs and his advocacy for nonviolent
resistance.

5- Who was the first emperor of Rome?
Augustus Caesar Augustus Caesar was
the first Roman emperor, and he ruled the
Roman Empire from 27 BC until his death in
14 AD. He was born Gaius Octavius, but
after Julius Caesar, his great-uncle and
adoptive father, was assassinated, he took
the name Augustus and became the sole
ruler of Rome.

Augustus is known for his military
conquests, political reforms, and promotion
of arts and culture. Under his rule, the

Roman Empire experienced a period of peace and stability known as the Pax Romana, which lasted for over 200 years.

1- What drink is Fermented from the sap of the agave plant?
a) Tequila
b) Rum

2- Made from the cacao tree?
a) Coffee
b) Hot Chocolate

3- Which beverage originated in Scotland and is made from malted barley, water, yeast, and hops?
a) Beer
b) Whiskey

4- Which beverage is made from the dried leaves of Camellia sinensis?
a) Green Tea
b) Herbal Tea

5- Made from fermented grape juice?
a) Wine
b) Beer

6- Brewed coffee served over ice?
a) Iced Coffee
b) Cold Brew

7- Which beverage is a carbonated soft drink that was first marketed as a tonic for various health benefits?
a) Coca-Cola
b) Sprite

8- Which beverage is a Japanese fermented tea that has a slightly sweet and sour taste?
a) Matcha
b) Kombucha

9- A caffeine-free alternative to coffee?
a) Chicory
b) Yerba Mate

10- Carbonated soft drink that is flavored with vanilla and other ingredients?
a) Root Beer
b) Cream Soda

ANSWERS:

1- Which beverage is made from the fermented sap of the agave plant?
Tequila Tequila is a type of distilled alcoholic beverage made from the blue agave plant, which is native to Mexico. It is named after the city of Tequila in the state of Jalisco, where the drink originated. Tequila is typically produced by steaming the agave plant and then fermenting and distilling the resulting juice.

It is often consumed as a shot with salt and lime, or used as a base for cocktails such as margaritas. In order to be considered true tequila, the drink must be produced in certain regions of Mexico and meet specific criteria established by the Mexican government.

2- Which beverage is made from roasted and ground seeds of the cacao tree?
Hot Chocolate. Hot chocolate, also known as cocoa, has been consumed for thousands of years. The Mayans and Aztecs were known to drink a bitter, spiced chocolate beverage that was believed to have medicinal properties. It wasn't until the 16th century that hot chocolate was introduced to Europe and sweetened with sugar or honey to make it more palatable.

3- Which beverage originated in Scotland and is made from malted barley, water, yeast, and hops?
Beer. Beer is one of the oldest and most widely consumed alcoholic beverages in the world, with evidence of its existence dating back to ancient civilizations such as Mesopotamia and Egypt. It is typically made from water, malted barley, hops, and yeast, and can come in a variety of styles such as lagers, ales, stouts, and porters. Beer is

also a significant part of many cultures and traditions, and is often associated with social gatherings and celebrations.

4- Which beverage is made from the dried leaves of Camellia sinensis?

Green Tea Green tea is a type of tea that is made from Camellia sinensis leaves and buds that have not undergone the same withering and oxidation process used to make black tea and oolong tea. It is believed to have originated in China over 4,000 years ago and has since become popular throughout Asia and the rest of the world.

Green tea is known for its high levels of antioxidants, specifically a type called catechins, which are believed to have numerous health benefits including reducing the risk of certain types of cancer and cardiovascular disease. Additionally, green tea contains caffeine and the amino acid L-theanine, which can help improve focus and relaxation.

5- Which beverage is made from fermented grape juice?

Wine Wine is an alcoholic beverage made from fermented grapes or other fruits. It has been produced and consumed for thousands of years, and is a significant part of many cultures and traditions. The process of winemaking involves crushing the grapes and fermenting the juice with yeast, which converts the sugar in the grapes into alcohol.

Wine can come in a variety of colors, including red, white, and rosé, and can be classified based on factors such as sweetness, acidity, and alcohol content. Additionally, wine is often aged in oak barrels, which can impart flavors and aromas such as vanilla, toast, and spice.

6- Which beverage is made from brewed coffee that is chilled or served over ice?
Iced Coffee Iced coffee is a popular variation of coffee that is served chilled or over ice. It is typically made by brewing hot coffee and then allowing it to cool, or by brewing coffee directly over ice. Iced coffee has been around for over a century, with records of it being served in Algeria as early as the 1840s.

It gained popularity in the United States in the 20th century, particularly during the hot summer months. Iced coffee can come in a variety of flavors and can be served with milk, cream, or sweeteners such as sugar or flavored syrups. Additionally, some people enjoy adding ice cream or other toppings to their iced coffee to create a dessert-like treat.

7- Which beverage is a carbonated soft drink that was first marketed as a tonic for various health benefits?

Coca-Cola Coca-Cola is one of the most popular soft drinks in the world and has been in production for over 135 years. It was first created by pharmacist John Pemberton in 1886 in Atlanta, Georgia, and was initially marketed as a medicine that could cure ailments such as headache, fatigue, and indigestion.

Coca-Cola's original formula contained cocaine, which was a common ingredient in medicinal products at the time, but the drug was removed from the recipe in 1903. Today, Coca-Cola is made from a combination of water, high fructose corn syrup or sugar, caffeine, phosphoric acid, caramel color, and natural flavorings. It is sold in over 200 countries and has become a symbol of American culture around the world.

8- Which beverage is a Japanese fermented tea that has a slightly sweet and sour taste?

Kombucha Kombucha is a fermented tea beverage that has become increasingly popular in recent years due to its potential health benefits. It is made by adding a symbiotic culture of bacteria and yeast (known as a SCOBY) to sweetened tea and allowing it to ferment for several days or weeks.

During the fermentation process, the bacteria and yeast consume the sugar in the tea, creating a fizzy, slightly sour drink that is low in alcohol and high in probiotics, organic acids, and antioxidants.

Kombucha has been claimed to have numerous health benefits, including improved digestion, immune system function, and mental clarity, although more research is needed to confirm these claims. Kombucha can also come in a variety of flavors, with ingredients such as fruits, herbs, and spices added to the fermentation process to create unique taste profiles.

9- Which beverage is made from the roots of the Coffea plant and is often used as a caffeine-free alternative to coffee?
Chicory Chicory is a plant that is part of the dandelion family and is known for its blue flowers and bitter leaves. It has been used for centuries as a medicinal herb and as a coffee substitute, particularly in Europe during times of coffee shortages.

Chicory root is roasted and ground to make a coffee-like beverage that is caffeine-free and has a slightly nutty, caramel-like flavor. Additionally, chicory leaves can be eaten raw or cooked and are a good source of vitamins and minerals such as vitamin C, vitamin K, and potassium. Chicory is also sometimes used in salads or as a garnish due to its attractive blue flowers.

10- Which beverage is a sweetened, carbonated soft drink that is flavored with vanilla and other ingredients?
Cream Soda Cream soda is a sweet carbonated soft drink that is flavored with vanilla or a similar flavor. It has a creamy texture and is typically light in color, often appearing clear or pale yellow.

Cream soda was first introduced in the United States in the 19th century and became popular as a soda fountain drink during the early 20th century. While the exact origins of cream soda are unclear, it is believed to have been inspired by Italian cream sodas, which were made with flavored syrups, cream, and carbonated water.

It can also be used as a mixer for cocktails or paired with ice cream to create a classic soda fountain treat.

1- Who is the author of the book "The Catcher in the Rye"?

2- What is the title of the first book in J.K. Rowling's Harry Potter series?

3- The fictional kingdom in J.R.R. Tolkien's "The Lord of the Rings"?

4- Who wrote the classic novel "To Kill a Mockingbird"?

5- The title of the first book in the "Chronicles of Narnia" series by C.S. Lewis?

6- Who wrote the novel "The Great Gatsby"?

7- What is the title of the novel by George Orwell that warns against totalitarianism?

8- What is the title of the novel by Ray Bradbury about a dystopian society that burns books?

9- Who wrote the epic poem "The Odyssey"?

10- What is the title of the novel by Gabriel García Márquez about a family in Colombia?

ANSWERS

1- Who is the author of the book "The Catcher in the Rye"?

J.D. Salinger J.D. Salinger was an American author who is best known for his novel "The Catcher in the Rye," which has become a literary classic and a cultural touchstone. The novel, which was first published in 1951, tells the story of Holden Caulfield, a troubled teenager who is expelled from his boarding school and goes on a journey of self-discovery in New York City.

"The Catcher in the Rye" has been widely praised for its authentic portrayal of teenage angst and alienation and its influence on subsequent generations of writers and readers. Salinger was famously reclusive and avoided the public eye for much of his life, rarely granting interviews or appearing in public. He died in 2010 at the age of 91.

2- What is the title of the first book in J.K. Rowling's Harry Potter series?
Harry Potter and the Philosopher's Stone (or Sorcerer's Stone in the US) "Harry Potter and the Philosopher's Stone" is the first book in the "Harry Potter" series, written by British author J.K. Rowling. It was first published in the United Kingdom in 1997 under the title "Harry Potter and the Philosopher's Stone," but was released as "Harry Potter and the Sorcerer's Stone" in the United States a year later.

The novel follows the story of Harry Potter, an orphaned boy who discovers on his eleventh birthday that he is a wizard and is invited to attend Hogwarts School of Witchcraft and Wizardry.

"Harry Potter and the Philosopher's Stone" has been a critical and commercial success, winning numerous awards and spawning a successful film franchise. It has also been credited with reigniting interest in reading among young people and has been translated into over 80 languages.

3- What is the name of the fictional kingdom in J.R.R. Tolkien's "The Lord of the Rings"?
Middle-earth **J.R.R.** Tolkien was an English writer, poet, and academic who is best known for his high fantasy novels "The Hobbit" and "The Lord of the Rings." Born in South Africa in 1892, Tolkien spent much of his childhood in England before serving in the British Army during World War I.

He went on to become a professor of Anglo-Saxon and English literature at Oxford University, where he developed a keen interest in mythology and language, which would later inform his fictional works.

Tolkien began writing "The Hobbit" in the 1930s, which was published in 1937 to critical acclaim. He followed it up with "The Lord of the Rings," which was published in three volumes between 1954 and 1955 and became a cultural phenomenon. Tolkien's works have since been adapted into numerous films, television shows, and video games, and have inspired generations of readers and writers alike.

4- Who wrote the classic novel "To Kill a Mockingbird"?

Harper Lee Harper Lee was an American author best known for her Pulitzer Prize-winning novel "To Kill a Mockingbird." The novel, which was first published in 1960, is a coming-of-age story set in the Deep South during the 1930s and deals with themes of racism, prejudice, and social inequality. "To

Kill a Mockingbird" has been widely praised for its powerful storytelling, nuanced characters, and insightful social commentary, and has become a classic of modern American literature. Despite the novel's enormous success, Lee remained private and largely avoided the public eye throughout her life. She published only one other novel, "Go Set a Watchman," in 2015, which was a controversial sequel to "To Kill a Mockingbird." Lee died in 2016 at the age of 89.

5- What is the title of the first book in the "Chronicles of Narnia" series by C.S. Lewis?

The Lion, the Witch and the Wardrobe

C.S. Lewis was a British writer and scholar who is best known for his fantasy novels, particularly "The Chronicles of Narnia" series. Born in Belfast, Northern Ireland in 1898, Lewis served in World War I and went on to become a professor of English literature at both Oxford and Cambridge Universities.

He was a prolific writer, producing works in a variety of genres, including science fiction, theology, and literary criticism, in addition to his famous fantasy novels. "The Chronicles of Narnia," which consists of seven books published between 1950 and 1956, has become a beloved classic of children's literature and has been adapted into numerous films, television shows, and stage productions.

Lewis's writing has been widely praised for its imaginative storytelling, strong moral themes, and vivid characters, and his influence can be seen in the works of many contemporary fantasy writers.

6- Who wrote the novel "The Great Gatsby"? F. Scott Fitzgerald F. Scott Fitzgerald was an American author and novelist who is best known for his classic novel "The Great Gatsby." Born in St. Paul, Minnesota in 1896, Fitzgerald was part of the "Lost Generation" of writers and artists who came of age during World War I and were disillusioned by the post-war era.

"The Great Gatsby," which was published in 1925, is a novel that explores themes of love, wealth, and the American Dream during the Roaring Twenties. Although initially receiving mixed reviews, the novel has since become a cultural touchstone and a classic of American literature.

Fitzgerald's writing style is often characterized by its lyrical prose and its ability to capture the zeitgeist of his era. Fitzgerald's personal life was marked by alcoholism and financial difficulties, and he died in 1940 at the age of 44.

7- What is the title of the novel by George Orwell that warns against totalitarianism? 1984 "1984" is a dystopian novel written by English author George Orwell and first published in 1949. The novel is set in a totalitarian society in the year 1984 and follows the story of Winston Smith, a low-ranking member of the ruling Party who begins to rebel against the government's strict control and surveillance.

The novel is famous for its portrayal of a bleak and oppressive society, as well as its depiction of government propaganda, censorship, and the manipulation of language.

The novel's concepts and themes, including the idea of "Big Brother" and the concept of "doublethink," have become iconic in popular culture and have been referenced in political discourse and literature for decades. "1984" continues to be widely read and studied today as a cautionary tale about the dangers of totalitarianism and the importance of individual freedom and autonomy.

8- What is the title of the novel by Ray Bradbury about a dystopian society that burns books? Fahrenheit 451 "Fahrenheit 451" is a dystopian novel written by American author Ray Bradbury and first published in 1953. The novel is set in a future society where books are banned and "firemen" are tasked with burning any that are found.

The novel follows the story of Guy Montag, a fireman who begins to question his role in society and becomes involved in a resistance movement to preserve and protect books.

The novel's title refers to the temperature at which paper burns, and its themes include censorship, the dangers of technology, and the power of knowledge and education. "Fahrenheit 451" has been widely praised for its vivid imagery, memorable characters, and thought-provoking ideas, and has become a classic of dystopian literature.

The novel has been adapted into numerous films, television shows, and stage productions, and continues to be studied and discussed in literature courses and book clubs around the world.

9- Who wrote the epic poem "The Odyssey"? Homer Homer is an ancient Greek poet who is traditionally credited with composing two of the greatest works of Western literature: the epic poems "The Iliad" and "The Odyssey." Little is known about Homer's life, and some scholars even debate whether he was a real historical figure or a legendary figure created to explain the authorship of these epic works.

"The Iliad" is an epic poem that tells the story of the Trojan War, while "The Odyssey" tells the story of Odysseus, a Greek hero who is trying to return home after the war. Both works are written in dactylic hexameter, a poetic meter commonly used in ancient Greek literature, and have been widely influential in literature and culture for thousands of years.

Homer's writing is known for its vivid imagery, powerful storytelling, and complex characters, and has had a profound impact on Western literature and culture.

10- What is the title of the novel by Gabriel García Márquez about a family in Colombia? One Hundred Years of Solitude Gabriel García Márquez was a Colombian novelist, journalist, and Nobel Prize winner who is widely regarded as one of the most influential Latin American writers of the 20th century. Born in Aracataca, Colombia in

1927, García Márquez was raised by his grandparents and grew up listening to their stories of the Colombian Caribbean region, which would later inspire much of his writing.

He is best known for his novels "One Hundred Years of Solitude" and "Love in the Time of Cholera," both of which are considered modern classics of literature. García Márquez's writing is known for its magical realism, a genre that blends the fantastical with the ordinary and is characterized by its rich imagery and vibrant language.

Throughout his career, García Márquez was a prominent advocate for social justice and political freedom, and his writing often addressed themes of colonialism, dictatorship, and social inequality. He died in 2014 at the age of 87, leaving behind a lasting legacy as one of the most celebrated writers of the 20th century.

1- What is the capital of Canada?

2- What is the name of the world's largest desert?

3- What is the smallest country in the world?

4- Which planet in our solar system is known for having the "Great Red Spot"?

5- What is the highest mountain in Africa?

6- Who discovered penicillin?

7- Which river is the longest in the world?

8- What is the smallest bone in the body?

9- Who painted "The Starry Night"?

10- What is the name of the world's largest ocean?

1- What is the capital of Canada?
Ottawa. Ottawa is the capital city of Canada, located in the eastern province of Ontario. The city was founded in 1826 as Bytown and was later renamed Ottawa in 1855. It was chosen as the capital of Canada in 1857 due to its central location between Montreal and Toronto, and its position on the Ottawa River.

Today, Ottawa is home to many national institutions and landmarks, including the Parliament Buildings, the National Gallery of Canada, and the Canadian Museum of History. The city is also known for its vibrant cultural scene, which includes numerous festivals, museums, and performing arts venues. Ottawa has a population of over 1 million people, making it the fourth-largest city in Canada, and is known for its high standard of living and quality of life.

2- What is the name of the world's largest desert?

The Sahara. The Sahara is the world's largest hot desert, covering approximately 3.6 million square miles (9.4 million square kilometers) across northern Africa. It stretches from the Atlantic Ocean in the west to the Red Sea in the east and from the Mediterranean Sea in the north to the Sahel region in the south.

The Sahara is known for its extreme heat, with temperatures sometimes reaching up to 136 degrees Fahrenheit (58 degrees Celsius) during the day, and its vast sand dunes, some of which can reach up to 600 feet (183 meters) in height.

Despite its harsh conditions, the Sahara is home to a diverse range of flora and fauna, including camels, desert foxes, and date palms. The Sahara has been inhabited by humans for thousands of years, with evidence of ancient civilizations and trade routes dating back to the Neolithic era. Today, the Sahara is a popular destination for tourists, who come to explore its stunning landscapes and experience its unique cultures and traditions.

3- What is the smallest country in the world? Vatican City Vatican City is an independent city-state located within Rome, Italy. It is the smallest country in the world, with a total area of only 0.17 square miles (0.44 square kilometers), and has a population of around 800 people, most of whom are members of the Catholic Church or work for the Vatican.

Vatican City is home to several important religious and cultural landmarks, including St. Peter's Basilica, the Sistine Chapel, and the Vatican Museums. It is also the headquarters of the Roman Catholic Church and the residence of the Pope, who serves as both the spiritual leader of the Catholic

Church and the head of state of Vatican City.
Vatican City has its own economy, postal system, and media outlets, and is recognized as a sovereign state by most countries in the world. It is a popular destination for tourists and pilgrims from around the world, who come to see its iconic landmarks and experience the rich history and culture of the Catholic Church.

4- Which planet in our solar system is known for having the "Great Red Spot"?
Jupiter Jupiter is the largest planet in our solar system, with a diameter of 86,881 miles (139,822 kilometers). It is named after the Roman king of gods and is known for its colorful and distinct cloud bands, its Great Red Spot, and its numerous moons.

Jupiter is a gas giant, consisting mainly of hydrogen and helium, and has a strong magnetic field that creates intense radiation belts around the planet. It is the fifth planet from the sun and has an average distance of 483.8 million miles (778.5 million kilometers) from it. Jupiter has a relatively short day, completing one rotation on its axis in just under 10 hours, which makes it the fastest-rotating planet in the solar system.

It also has a strong gravitational influence on other planets and objects in the solar system, which has helped to shape their orbits and movements over time. Jupiter has been studied extensively by space missions, including the Voyager and Galileo spacecraft, and continues to be a focus of scientific research and discovery.

5- What is the highest mountain in Africa?

Mount Kilimanjaro Mount Kilimanjaro is the highest mountain in Africa, with a peak that rises to 19,341 feet (5,895 meters) above sea level. It is located in Tanzania, near the border with Kenya, and is composed of three distinct volcanic cones: Kibo, Mawenzi, and Shira. Kilimanjaro is a dormant volcano, with its last major eruption occurring about 360,000 years ago.

The mountain is known for its diverse ecosystems, ranging from lush rainforest at the base to Arctic-like conditions near the summit, and is home to a variety of wildlife, including elephants, buffalo, and primates. Kilimanjaro is a popular destination for hikers and climbers from around the world, who come to experience its stunning scenery and challenge themselves to reach its summit.

Despite its high altitude, Kilimanjaro is considered to be one of the most accessible of the world's major peaks, with no technical climbing skills required to reach its summit. However, climbers still need to be well-prepared and acclimatized to the altitude, as the summit can be a challenging and dangerous ascent.

6- Who is credited with the discovery of penicillin?

Alexander Fleming Alexander Fleming was a Scottish microbiologist who is credited with the discovery of penicillin, one of the world's first antibiotics. In 1928, while working at St. Mary's Hospital in London, Fleming observed that a mold called Penicillium notatum had contaminated one of his petri dishes, and that the bacteria surrounding the mold had been killed off.

This discovery led him to further research and develop the first antibiotic from the mold, which he named penicillin. Penicillin was a major breakthrough in the treatment of bacterial infections and has saved countless lives since its discovery. Fleming was awarded the Nobel Prize in Physiology or Medicine in 1945, along with two other scientists, for his work on penicillin.

Despite his major contribution to medicine, Fleming was known for his modesty and dedication to his work, and is often quoted as saying, "One sometimes finds what one is not looking for."

7- Which river is the longest in the world?
Nile The Nile River is the longest river in the world, stretching over 4,135 miles (6,650 kilometers) through 11 countries in northeastern Africa.

The river has two main tributaries: the White Nile, which originates in Lake Victoria in Tanzania and flows northward through Uganda and Sudan, and the Blue Nile, which originates in Ethiopia and flows westward to meet the White Nile in Sudan.

The Nile has played a significant role in the development of ancient and modern civilizations, providing water and fertile land for agriculture.

The ancient Egyptian civilization, in particular, was closely tied to the Nile, as its annual flooding deposited nutrient-rich silt on the river banks, enabling the growth of crops.

Today, the Nile remains a vital source of water and food for millions of people living along its banks, and is a major transportation route for goods and people in the region.

8- What is the smallest bone in the human body? The stirrup bone (or stapes) in the ear. The stirrup bone, also known as the stapes, is the smallest bone in the human body. It is one of three bones in the middle ear, along with the malleus and incus, and plays a crucial role in hearing.

The stapes is only about 2.8 millimeters long in adults and weighs just a few milligrams. Despite its small size, the stapes is incredibly strong and is able to transmit sound vibrations from the eardrum to the inner ear. Interestingly, the stapes bone is believed to have evolved from a bone in the jaw of early reptiles, which gradually migrated into the middle ear as reptiles evolved into mammals.

The stapes bone is therefore a fascinating example of how evolution has repurposed existing structures to serve new functions over time.

9- Who painted the famous work of art called "The Starry Night"? Vincent van Gogh. "The Starry Night" is a famous oil painting by the Dutch artist Vincent van Gogh, created in 1889 while he was a patient at the Saint-Paul-de-Mausole asylum in France.

The painting depicts the view from his window at the asylum, looking out over the village of Saint-Rémy-de-Provence and the Alpilles mountains. Van Gogh's distinctive style is evident in the swirling, stylized forms of the stars and the village below, as well as the bold use of color and thick brushstrokes.

"The Starry Night" is considered one of van Gogh's most iconic works, and has become one of the most recognized and reproduced paintings in the world. It is housed in the Museum of Modern Art in New York City, where it is one of the most popular works in the museum's collection.

10- What is the name of the world's largest ocean? The Pacific Ocean. The Pacific Ocean is the largest and deepest ocean on Earth, covering an area of approximately 63.8 million square miles (165.25 million square kilometers) and containing more than half of the world's free water.

It stretches from the Arctic Ocean in the north to the Southern Ocean in the south, and is bounded by the Americas to the east and Asia and Australia to the west. The deepest part of the ocean, the Mariana Trench, is located in the western Pacific and reaches a depth of 36,070 feet (10,994 meters).

The Pacific Ocean is also known for its "Ring of Fire," a horseshoe-shaped region around its edges where many active volcanoes and frequent earthquakes occur due to tectonic activity.

The Pacific Ocean plays a critical role in regulating the Earth's climate and weather patterns, and is an important source of food, transportation, and natural resources for people around the world.

1- What is the only continent that does not have a desert?
a) North America
b) Europe

2- In which year was the first electric car invented?
a) 1884
b) 1954

3- What is the most common blood type in the world?
a) AB+
b) O+

4- What is the smallest breed of dog?
a) Chihuahua
b) Dachshund

5- How many taste buds does an average human tongue have?
a) 500
b) 10,000

6- What is the name of the deepest known point in the ocean?
a) Mariana Trench
b) Puerto Rico Trench

7- What is the name of the tallest waterfall in the world?
a) Angel Falls
b) Victoria Falls

8- What is the only bird that can fly backward?
a) Hummingbird
b) Ostrich

9- In which country was the first university established?
a) Italy
b) Egypt

10- What is the longest venomous snake in the world?
a) King Cobra
b) Black Mamba

ANSWERS:

1- What is the only continent that does not have a desert? Europe. Europe is the second-smallest continent on Earth, covering an area of approximately 10.18 million square kilometers (3.93 million square miles), which is roughly 6.7% of the Earth's total land area. However, it is the third-most populous continent, with an estimated population of over 747 million people as of 2021.

Europe is bordered by the Arctic Ocean to the north, the Atlantic Ocean to the west, and the Mediterranean Sea to the south. It is home to some of the world's oldest and most influential civilizations, including Ancient Greece, the Roman Empire, and the Renaissance period. The continent is also known for its diverse cultures, languages, and historical landmarks, such as the Eiffel Tower in Paris, the Colosseum in Rome, and the Acropolis in Athens.

Europe is a major economic power, with many of the world's largest economies, and it has played a significant role in global politics and international relations for centuries.

2- In which year was the first electric car invented? 1884 The first practical electric car was invented in 1884 by Thomas Parker, a British inventor who was responsible for electrifying the London Underground. Parker's electric car was powered by a rechargeable battery and had a range of about 50 miles (80 kilometers) on a single charge.

It was used primarily as a taxi in London, but its high cost and limited range made it impractical for widespread use. However, Parker's invention laid the groundwork for future electric cars, and in the early 1900s, electric cars were popular in many cities due to their quiet operation and lack of exhaust emissions.

The development of the internal combustion engine and the availability of cheap gasoline eventually led to the decline of electric cars, but in recent years, the rise of electric vehicle technology has renewed interest in electric cars as a sustainable alternative to traditional gasoline-powered cars.

3- What is the most common blood type in the world? O+ Blood type O+ is the most common blood type among people worldwide, accounting for about 38% of the population. This blood type is characterized by the presence of both O antigens and Rh factor on the surface of red blood cells.

People with O+ blood are often referred to as universal donors because their blood can be transfused to people with any blood type that is Rh-positive, while they can only receive blood from people with O+ or O- blood types. In addition to being a universal donor, O+ blood type is also associated with a lower risk of heart disease and certain types of cancer, although the reasons for this are not entirely clear.

However, people with O+ blood type may be more susceptible to certain infections, such as malaria and cholera, than people with other blood types.

4- What is the smallest breed of dog?
Chihuahua The Chihuahua is the smallest dog breed in the world, with an average weight of just 2-6 pounds (1-3 kilograms) and a height of 6-9 inches (15-23 centimeters) at the shoulder. The breed is named after the state of Chihuahua in Mexico, where it is believed to have originated.

Despite their small size, Chihuahuas are known for their big personalities and can be quite feisty and protective. They are also loyal and affectionate with their owners, and make excellent lap dogs. Chihuahuas are often seen as a fashion accessory due to their small size and adorable appearance, and have been popularized by celebrity owners such as Paris Hilton and Britney Spears.

However, it's important to remember that Chihuahuas, like all dogs, require proper training and socialization to be well-behaved companions.

5- How many taste buds does an average human tongue have? 10,000 The human tongue is a muscular organ that is located in the mouth and plays an important role in speech and taste. It is made up of eight muscles, which work together to move the tongue in all directions. The tongue is covered in thousands of taste buds, which are specialized cells that allow us to perceive different tastes, such as sweet, sour, salty, and bitter.

Interestingly, taste buds are not only found on the tongue, but also on the roof of the mouth, the back of the throat, and even in the esophagus. The tongue also helps to mix food with saliva and push it towards the back of the mouth for swallowing.

Additionally, the tongue plays a role in shaping sounds and movements of the mouth for speech, making it a key part of communication.

6- What is the name of the deepest known point in the ocean? Mariana Trench. The Mariana Trench is the deepest known part of the world's oceans, with a maximum depth of approximately 36,070 feet (10,994 meters). It is located in the western Pacific Ocean, to the east of the Mariana Islands, and is named after them.

The Mariana Trench is a crescent-shaped trench that extends for more than 1,550 miles (2,500 kilometers) and is part of the

Pacific Ring of Fire, a region of frequent seismic and volcanic activity. The pressure at the bottom of the Mariana Trench is estimated to be more than 8 tons per square inch (1,125 kg per square cm), which is more than 1,000 times the pressure at sea level.

Despite the extreme conditions, the Mariana Trench is home to a variety of unique and fascinating organisms, including some that are bioluminescent (able to produce their own light) to help them navigate in the darkness.

7- What is the name of the tallest waterfall in the world? Angel Falls. Angel Falls is the highest waterfall in the world, with a total height of 3,212 feet (979 meters) and a continuous drop of 2,648 feet (807 meters). It is located in Canaima National Park in the Gran Sabana region of Venezuela, and is named after the

American aviator Jimmie Angel, who was the first person to fly over it in 1933.
The waterfall is formed by the waters of the Churun River, which plunge over the edge of Auyantepui mountain in a single freefall. Due to its remote location and difficult access, Angel Falls was not officially discovered until 1935, and it remained largely unknown to the outside world until the mid-20th century.

Today, it is a popular tourist attraction and is considered one of the natural wonders of the world.

8- What is the only bird that can fly backward? Hummingbird Hummingbirds are the smallest birds in the world, with the smallest species weighing less than a penny. They are also the only birds that can fly backwards and hover in mid-air, thanks to their unique wing structure that allows them to beat their wings up to 80 times per second.

Hummingbirds are found only in the Americas, from Alaska to Tierra del Fuego, and are known for their bright and iridescent feathers. They have a high metabolism and need to consume up to half their body weight in nectar every day to maintain their energy levels, which is why they have a long, slender bill and a tongue that is shaped like a straw to extract nectar from flowers.

Despite their small size, hummingbirds are highly intelligent and have excellent memory and spatial awareness, which helps them to navigate their environment and locate sources of food.

9- In which country was the first university established? b) Italy The first university established in the world is the University of Bologna, which was founded in 1088 in the city of Bologna, Italy. Originally known as the Studium, it was primarily a school of law and was established by a group of scholars who had gathered in Bologna to study the ancient Roman legal system.

Over time, the University of Bologna became one of the most prestigious institutions of higher learning in Europe and played a significant role in the development of modern science, medicine, and the arts. Some of its most famous alumni include the mathematician Leonardo Fibonacci, the philosopher Thomas Aquinas, and the artist Albrecht Dürer.

Today, the University of Bologna is still in operation and is one of the oldest and most respected universities in the world.

10- What is the longest venomous snake in the world? Black Mamba The Black Mamba is a species of venomous snake that is found in sub-Saharan Africa. It is considered to be one of the most dangerous snakes in the world, and is responsible for a large number of snakebite fatalities in Africa. The Black Mamba gets its name from the dark color of the inside of its mouth, which it displays as a warning before striking.

It can grow up to 14 feet in length and can move at speeds of up to 12 miles per hour, making it one of the fastest snakes in the world. The venom of the Black Mamba is highly toxic and can cause paralysis and death within a matter of hours if left untreated.

Despite its reputation, the Black Mamba is an important predator in its ecosystem and helps to control rodent populations.

1- What is the meaning of the Spanish
word "adios"?

2- Who wrote the famous novel "Don
Quixote"?

3- What is the name of the Spanish
dance that involves a group of people
stomping their feet and clapping their
hands?

4- Which Spanish painter is known for
his surrealist works, including "The
Persistence of Memory"?

5- What is the name of the Spanish royal
family?

6- What is the name of the Spanish
language television network that is
based in the United States?

7- What is the name of the Spanish island chain located off the coast of Africa?

8- Which Spanish tennis player has won a record 20 Grand Slam singles titles?

9- What is the name of the Spanish festival that takes place each year in Valencia, where participants throw tomatoes at each other?

ANSWERS:

1- What is the meaning of the Spanish word "adios"? Goodbye or farewell. The Spanish word "adios" is a common way of saying "goodbye" in Spanish. It comes from the phrase "a Dios" which means "to God." This phrase was originally used to wish someone a safe journey and to ask for God's protection during their travels.

Over time, the phrase was shortened to "adios" and became a standard part of the Spanish language. The word is commonly used in formal and informal situations, and is often accompanied by a gesture such as a wave or a handshake.

2- Wrote the famous novel "Don Quixote"? Miguel de Cervantes. Miguel de Cervantes was a Spanish writer and author of the famous novel "Don Quixote," which is considered one of the most important works of Spanish literature and a masterpiece of world literature.

Despite being a significant figure in the literary world, Cervantes faced financial difficulties throughout his life and was imprisoned multiple times for various reasons.

3- What is the name of the Spanish dance that involves a group of people stomping their feet and clapping their hands? Flamenco. Flamenco is a traditional dance form from Andalusia, a southern region of Spain. It is a highly expressive dance that combines rhythmic footwork, hand clapping, finger snapping, and intricate arm and body movements, often accompanied by live music and singing.

Flamenco is considered a cultural expression of the Andalusian gypsy community, although its exact origins are uncertain and likely have influences from various cultures, such as Arabic, Jewish, and Spanish.

Flamenco has become popular worldwide and is recognized as an Intangible Cultural Heritage of Humanity by UNESCO.

4- Known for his surrealist works, including "The Persistence of Memory"? Salvador Dali. Salvador Dali was a Spanish surrealist artist known for his bizarre, dreamlike paintings that often incorporated bizarre and unexpected images. He was also a master of self-promotion and was known for his flamboyant personality and eccentric behavior, often dressing in elaborate outfits and appearing in public with a pet ocelot.

Despite his controversial reputation, Dali remains one of the most famous and influential artists of the 20th century, with his works being exhibited in major museums and galleries around the world.

5- What is the name of the Spanish royal family? The House of Bourbon The House of Bourbon is a European royal dynasty that originated in France in the 16th century and has since ruled over various countries, including Spain, Naples, and Sicily.

The dynasty was founded by Henry IV of France, who was known for his political and military skills and for his conversion to Catholicism. Over the centuries, the House of Bourbon has played a significant role in European history, and its members have included many notable figures, including Louis XIV of France, Philip V of Spain, and Charles III of Spain.
Today, the Bourbon dynasty continues to exist, with members of the family holding various titles and positions of influence throughout Europe.

6- What is the name of the Spanish language television network that is based in the United States?
Univision Univision is a Spanish-language television network in the United States that was founded in 1962. It is the largest Spanish-language network in the country and reaches approximately 85% of Hispanic households in the US.

Univision's programming includes news, sports, telenovelas (Spanish-language soap operas), and other entertainment shows.

The network has been a significant cultural influence for the Hispanic community in the US, and its coverage of events like the World Cup and the Olympic Games is widely watched by Spanish-speaking audiences. In recent years, Univision has expanded its digital presence, launching streaming services and mobile apps to reach younger audiences.

7- What is the name of the Spanish island chain located off the coast of Africa? The Canary Islands The Canary Islands are a Spanish archipelago located off the northwest coast of Africa. The islands are known for their unique flora and fauna, with a number of endemic species found only in the Canary Islands. The islands are also home to several world-renowned astronomical observatories due to their clear skies and favorable location.

The Canary Islands are a popular tourist destination, with millions of visitors each year attracted to the islands' beaches, natural parks, and cultural attractions. Despite being part of Spain, the Canary Islands have a distinct culture and history, influenced by their location and history as a stopover point for ships traveling between Europe and the Americas.

8- Which Spanish tennis player has won a record 20 Grand Slam singles titles? Rafael Nadal Rafael Nadal is a Spanish professional tennis player widely regarded as one of the greatest players of all time. He has won 20 Grand Slam singles titles, tying the record held by Roger Federer, and has also won two Olympic gold medals in singles and one in doubles.

Nadal has a remarkable record on clay courts, having won 13 French Open titles, the most of any player in history. In addition to his success on the court, Nadal is also known for his sportsmanship and humility, earning him a reputation as a beloved figure in the world of tennis.

9- What is the name of the Spanish festival that takes place each year in Valencia, where participants throw tomatoes at each other? La Tomatina La Tomatina is an annual festival that takes place in the town of Buñol, near Valencia,

Spain. It involves thousands of people throwing ripe tomatoes at each other in the streets.

The festival has been held since 1945 and is now a major tourist attraction, with participants coming from all over the world.

1- Who played the character of Iron Man in the Marvel Cinematic Universe movies?

2- Which iconic artist released the hit song "Thriller" in 1984?

3- Who won the Best Actress award at the 2021 Oscars for her role in the movie "Nomadland"?.

4- What is the name of the lead character in the TV series "Breaking Bad"?

5- Which famous singer played the character of Ally in the 2018 movie "A Star is Born"?

6- Which movie won the Best Picture award at the 2021 Oscars?

7- Who is the author of the Harry Potter book series?

8- Which TV show features the characters Rachel, Monica, Phoebe, Chandler, Ross, and Joey?

9- Who played the character of Neo in the movie "The Matrix"?

10 - Which movie did Leonardo DiCaprio win his first Academy Award for Best Actor in a Leading Role?

ANSWERS:

1- Who played the character of Iron Man in the Marvel Cinematic Universe movies? Robert Downey Jr. Iron Man is a fictional superhero character created by Marvel Comics. The character, whose real name is Tony Stark, made his first appearance in 1963. He is known for his high-tech suit of armor, which gives him superhuman strength and the ability to fly.

The character has been adapted into various films and TV shows, with actor Robert Downey Jr. playing the role in the Marvel Cinematic Universe films.

2- Which iconic artist released the hit song "Thriller" in 1984? Michael Jackson. Michael Jackson, also known as the "King of Pop," is one of the most successful musicians of all time. He has sold over 350 million records worldwide and is known for his hits such as "Thriller," "Beat It," and "Billie Jean." Jackson also popularized iconic dance moves such as the moonwalk and the robot dance.

3- Who won the Best Actress award at the 2021 Oscars for her role in the movie "Nomadland"? Frances McDormand.
Frances McDormand is a highly acclaimed American actress who has won numerous awards throughout her career, including an Academy Award, a Tony Award, and two Golden Globe Awards.

She is known for her versatile acting abilities and has starred in a wide variety of films, from dramas to comedies, including Fargo, Three Billboards Outside Ebbing, Missouri, and Almost Famous.

McDormand is also a prominent advocate for women in the entertainment industry and has been outspoken about the need for greater diversity and representation in Hollywood.

4- What is the name of the lead character in the TV series "Breaking Bad"? Walter White. Walter White is a fictional character in the television series "Breaking Bad." He is portrayed as a high school chemistry teacher who, after being diagnosed with cancer, begins producing and selling methamphetamine in order to secure his family's financial future after his death.

The character was created and developed by Vince Gilligan and is played by actor Bryan Cranston.

5- Which famous singer played the character of Ally in the 2018 movie "A Star is Born"? Lady Gaga. "A Star is Born" is a movie that has been remade four times, in 1937, 1954, 1976, and 2018, with each version having a slightly different storyline and different actors in the lead roles.

Lady Gaga is an American singer, songwriter, and actress. She has won numerous awards throughout her career, including 12 Grammy Awards, 1 Academy Award, and 3 Brit Awards. She is also known for her philanthropic work and activism on behalf of the LGBTQ+ community, mental health, and various other social and political causes.

6- Which movie won the Best Picture award at the 2021 Oscars? "Nomadland".
Nomadland is a 2020 American drama film directed by Chloé Zhao, based on the non-fiction book "Nomadland: Surviving America in the Twenty-First Century" by Jessica Bruder. The film stars Frances McDormand as a woman in her 60s who, after losing everything in the Great Recession, embarks on a journey through the American West, living as a modern-day nomad in a van.

The film won several awards, including Best Picture, Best Director, and Best Actress (McDormand) at the 93rd Academy Awards.

7- Who is the author of Harry Potter?
J.K. Rowling. J.K. Rowling, born on July 31, 1965, is a British author best known for writing the Harry Potter series. She wrote the first Harry Potter book, "Harry Potter and the Philosopher's Stone," in cafes in Edinburgh, Scotland, while she was living on welfare.

The book was initially rejected by several publishers before being accepted by Bloomsbury, and it went on to become a global phenomenon, with over 500 million copies sold in 80 languages. Rowling is also known for her philanthropic work and activism, including her support for multiple sclerosis research and her outspoken stance on various political and social issues.

8- Which TV show features the characters Rachel, Monica, Phoebe, Chandler, Ross, and Joey? "Friends". One fact about the TV show "Friends" is that it was originally titled "Insomnia Cafe" and was going to be set entirely in a coffee shop. The creators, David Crane and Marta Kauffman, eventually expanded the concept to include a diverse group of six friends and renamed the show to "Friends."

The show premiered on September 22, 1994, and became a cultural phenomenon, running for ten seasons and winning numerous awards.

9- Who played the character of Neo in the movie "The Matrix"? Keanu Reeves. Keanu Reeves, born in Beirut, Lebanon in 1964, is a Canadian actor known for his roles in movies such as "The Matrix" trilogy, "John Wick" series, and "Speed."

Despite his success in Hollywood, Reeves is known for his humble and down-to-earth personality and is often praised for his generosity and philanthropy. He has donated millions of dollars to various charities and causes, including cancer research and children's hospitals.

10- Which movie did Leonardo DiCaprio win his first Academy Award for Best Actor in a Leading Role? "The Revenant" (2015) "The Revenant" was directed by Alejandro González Iñárritu and stars Leonardo DiCaprio, who won the Academy Award for Best Actor for his role in the film. The movie is known for its grueling production, with the cast and crew enduring extreme weather

conditions and challenging filming locations
to bring the story of frontiersman Hugh
Glass to life.

The film was also praised for its
cinematography, with Emmanuel Lubezki
winning his third consecutive Oscar for Best
Cinematography for his work on the film.

1- Who is the lead singer of the band Coldplay?
Chris Evans
Chris Martin

2- Who is the creator of the famous character Sherlock Holmes?
Charles Dickens
Arthur Conan Doyle

3- Who is the current CEO of Tesla and SpaceX?
Mark Zuckerberg
Elon Musk

4- Who was the lead singer of the band Queen?
Feddie Mercury
David Bowie

5- Who is the first person to step on the moon?
Neil Armstrong
Buzz Aldrin

6- Who is the lead actor in the movie "Forrest Gump"?
Tom Hanks
Brad Pitt

7- Who is the founder of Microsoft Corporation?
Bill Gates
Steve Jobs

ANSWERS:

1- Who is the lead singer of the band Coldplay? Chris Martin Chris Martin is the lead singer and co-founder of the British rock band Coldplay, which has sold over 100 million records worldwide and won numerous awards, including seven Grammy Awards.

Martin is also known for his philanthropic work and activism, supporting causes such as poverty reduction, climate change, and refugee rights.

2- Who is the creator of the famous character Sherlock Holmes? Arthur Conan Doyle. Arthur Conan Doyle is that he initially studied medicine and worked as a doctor, but he eventually gave up his medical practice to become a full-time writer.

3- Who is the current CEO of Tesla and SpaceX? Elon Musk Elon Musk is the founder and CEO of SpaceX, a company that designs and manufactures rockets for space exploration and transportation. SpaceX has successfully launched multiple missions to the International Space Station and has plans to send humans to Mars in the future.

4- Who was the lead singer of the band Queen? Freddie Mercury Freddie Mercury was born Farrokh Bulsara in Stone Town, Zanzibar (now Tanzania) and later changed his name when he became the lead singer of the rock band Queen. He is widely regarded as one of the greatest singers in the history of rock music and is known for his flamboyant stage presence and vocal range.

5- Who is the first person to step on the moon? Neil Armstrong Neil Armstrong was the first person to step on the moon. On July 20, 1969, Armstrong, along with Buzz Aldrin, landed the Apollo 11 spacecraft on the moon's surface and Armstrong famously uttered the phrase, "That's one small step for man, one giant leap for mankind," as he became the first human to step on the moon.

6- Who is the lead actor in the movie "Forrest Gump"? Tom Hanks Tom Hanks is one of the few actors to have won the Academy Award for Best Actor in consecutive years. He won the award in 1993 for his role in "Philadelphia" and again in 1994 for his role in "Forrest Gump." Hanks is widely regarded as one of the greatest actors of his generation and has appeared in numerous critically acclaimed films throughout his career.

7- Who is the founder of Microsoft Corporation? Bill Gates Microsoft Corporation became the world's largest personal-computer software company. Gates, along with Paul Allen, started Microsoft in 1975, and the company played a key role in the development of the personal computer industry. Gates is also known for his philanthropic work, particularly through the Bill and Melinda Gates Foundation, which focuses on global health and education initiatives.

1- What is the average body temperature of a healthy cat?
A. 99.5-102.5°F
B. 96.5-99.5°F
2- What is the name for a cat's flexible spine that allows it to contort into tight spaces?
A. Hyperflexion
B. Supercat power

3- What is the name for a cat's hunting instinct?
A. Prey drive
B. Flight instinct

4- What is the term for a cat's fear of water?
A. Hydrophobia
B. Aquaphobia

5- What is the name for a cat's third eyelid?
A. Nictitating membrane
B. Iris

6- What is the name for a cat's retractable claws?
A. Digitigrade
B. Feliniform

7- What is the term for a cat's loud, intense purring that is often accompanied by kneading?
A. Purr box
B. Power purr

8- What is the name for a male cat that has not been neutered?
A. Tom
B. Jerry

1- What is the average body temperature of a healthy cat?

A. 99.5-102.5°F
Cats have a higher average body temperature than humans, with a range of 99.5-102.5°F. A healthy cat's body temperature can fluctuate slightly throughout the day but should remain within this range. A body temperature below 96.5°F or above 104°F may indicate a medical problem and should be evaluated by a veterinarian.

2- What is the name for a cat's flexible spine that allows it to contort into tight spaces?

A. Hyperflexion
A cat's spine is highly flexible due to the presence of numerous small bones and intervertebral discs. This flexibility allows cats to contort their bodies in ways that seem impossible to humans, such as squeezing into tight spaces or twisting to land on their feet when falling. The ability to bend and twist like this is sometimes called hyperflexion.

3- What is the name for a cat's hunting instinct?

A. Prey drive
Cats are natural predators with a strong instinct to hunt and capture prey. This instinct is often referred to as prey drive and is exhibited by behaviors such as stalking, pouncing, and playing with toys. While not

all cats exhibit the same level of prey drive, it is a common characteristic of the species.

4- What is the term for a cat's fear of water?

B. Aquaphobia
While the term "hydrophobia" is often used to describe a fear of water, it actually refers specifically to a fear of rabies. The term for a fear of water in general is "aquaphobia." While many cats may not enjoy getting wet, not all of them are necessarily afraid of water.

5- What is the name for a cat's third eyelid?

A. Nictitating membrane
A cat's third eyelid, also known as the nictitating membrane, is a thin, translucent membrane that is located on the inside corner of the eye. It is used to protect and moisten the eye, as well as to remove debris and irritants. While the third eyelid is normally hidden, it can become visible when a cat is sick or stressed.
Pronounced: nik-tuh-tey-ting.

6- What is the name for a cat's retractable claws?

B. Feliniform
While the term "digitigrade" is used to describe an animal that walks on its toes, it is not specifically related to a cat's retractable claws. The correct term for a cat's retractable claws is "feliniform." Cats are able to retract their claws to keep them sharp and prevent damage to the claws and paw pads.

7- What is the term for a cat's loud, intense purring that is often accompanied by kneading?

B. Power purr
The term "power purr" is used to describe a cat's loud, intense purring that is often accompanied by kneading. This behavior is usually a sign of contentment and relaxation and is sometimes referred to as "making

biscuits." While not all cats exhibit this behavior, it is common among many breeds.

8- What is the name for a male cat that has not been neutered?

A. Tom
A male cat that has not been neutered is often referred to as a "tom" or "tomcat."

1- What is the name of the cheese that is made from goat's milk?
A) Chevre
B) Roquefort

2- What is the name of the cheese that is made from sheep's milk?
A) Parmesan
B) Pecorino)

3- What is the name of the cheese that is made from cow's milk and is often used on pizza?
A) Gouda
B) Mozzarella)

4- What is the name of the cheese that is made from cow's milk and has holes in it?
A) Swiss)
B) Cheddar

5- What is the name of the cheese that is made from buffalo's milk and is often used in Italian cuisine?
A) Brie
B) Buffalo mozzarella

6- What is the name of the cheese that is made from sheep's milk and is often used in Greek cuisine?
A) Feta)
B) Camembert

7- What is the name of the cheese that is made from goat's milk and is often used in French cuisine?
A) Cheddar
B) Chevre)

8- What is the name of the cheese that is made from cow's milk and is often used in Mexican cuisine?
A) Cheddar
B) Queso fresco

9- What is the name of the cheese that is made from sheep's milk and is often used in Spanish cuisine?
A) Gouda
B) Manchego

10- What is the name of the cheese that is made from cow's milk and is often used in English cuisine?
A) Brie
B) Cheddar

11- What is the name of the cheese that is made from goat's milk and is often used in Moroccan cuisine?
A) Halloumi
B) Chèvre

12- What is the name of the cheese that is made from sheep's milk and is often used in Italian cuisine?
A) Pecorino
B) Gouda

13- What is the name of the cheese that is made from cow's milk and is often used in French cuisine?

A) Camembert

B) Monterey Jack

14- What is the name of the cheese that is made from sheep's milk and is often used in Turkish cuisine?

A) Gouda

B) Feta

15- What is the name of the cheese that is made from cow's milk and is often used in Swiss cuisine?

A) Raclette

B) Havarti

16- What is the name of the cheese that is made from goat's milk and is often used in Spanish cuisine?

A) Cheddar

B) Cabrales

17- What is the name of the cheese that is made from cow's milk and is often used in American cuisine?
A) Monterey Jack
B) Brie

18- What is the name of the cheese that is made from sheep's milk and is often used in Greek cuisine?
A) Halloumi
B) Kefalotyri

19- What is the name of the cheese that is made from cow's milk and is often used in German cuisine?
A) Camembert
B) Butterkäse

20- What is the name of the cheese that is made from goat's milk and is often used in Italian cuisine?
A) Ricotta
B) Caprino

21- What is the name of the cheese that is made from cow's milk and is often used in Dutch cuisine?
A) Edam
B) Blue cheese

ANSWERS

1- What is the name of the cheese that is made from goat's milk?
A) Chevre (Answer)
B) Roquefort

2- What is the name of the cheese that is made from sheep's milk?
A) Parmesan
B) Pecorino (Answer)

3- What is the name of the cheese that is made from cow's milk and is often used on pizza?
A) Gouda
B) Mozzarella (Answer)

4- What is the name of the cheese that is made from cow's milk and has holes in it?
A) Swiss (Answer)
B) Cheddar

5- What is the name of the cheese that is made from buffalo's milk and is often used in Italian cuisine?
A) Brie
B) Buffalo mozzarella (Answer)

6- What is the name of the cheese that is made from sheep's milk and is often used in Greek cuisine?
A) Feta (Answer)
B) Camembert

7- What is the name of the cheese that is made from goat's milk and is often used in French cuisine?
A) Cheddar
B) Chevre (Answer)

8- What is the name of the cheese that is made from cow's milk and is often used in Mexican cuisine?
A) Cheddar
B) Queso fresco (Answer)

9- What is the name of the cheese that is made from sheep's milk and is often used in Spanish cuisine?
A) Gouda
B) Manchego (Answer)

10- What is the name of the cheese that is made from cow's milk and is often used in English cuisine?
A) Brie
B) Cheddar (Answer)

11- What is the name of the cheese that is made from goat's milk and is often used in Moroccan cuisine?
A) Halloumi
B) Chèvre (Answer)

12- What is the name of the cheese that is made from sheep's milk and is often used in Italian cuisine?
A) Pecorino (Answer)
B) Gouda

13- What is the name of the cheese that is made from cow's milk and is often used in French cuisine?

A) Camembert (Answer)

B) Monterey Jack

14- What is the name of the cheese that is made from sheep's milk and is often used in Turkish cuisine?

A) Gouda

B) Feta (Answer)

15- What is the name of the cheese that is made from cow's milk and is often used in Swiss cuisine?

A) Raclette (Answer)

B) Havarti

16- What is the name of the cheese that is made from goat's milk and is often used in Spanish cuisine?

A) Cheddar

B) Cabrales (Answer)

17- What is the name of the cheese that is made from cow's milk and is often used in American cuisine?
A) Monterey Jack (Answer)
B) Brie

18- What is the name of the cheese that is made from sheep's milk and is often used in Greek cuisine?
A) Halloumi
B) Kefalotyri (Answer)

19- What is the name of the cheese that is made from cow's milk and is often used in German cuisine?
A) Camembert
B) Butterkäse (Answer)

20- What is the name of the cheese that is made from goat's milk and is often used in Italian cuisine?
A) Ricotta
B) Caprino (Answer)

21- What is the name of the cheese that is made from cow's milk and is often used in Dutch cuisine?
A) Edam (Answer)
B) Blue cheese

What does the idiom "Storm in a teacup" mean?

The idiom "storm in a teapot" refers to a situation that is blown out of proportion, causing an excessive amount of fuss or drama over a minor issue. It implies that the situation is small and insignificant, like a storm that occurs within the confined space of a teapot, rather than a significant event that requires a large-scale response.

The phrase is often used to describe situations where people are making a big deal out of something that really doesn't matter in the grand scheme of things. For example, if someone is getting overly upset about a minor mistake or inconvenience, you might say that they're making a "storm in a teapot."

Overall, the idiom "storm in a teapot" suggests that the issue is much ado about nothing and is not worth the attention or energy that it is receiving.